Mar-Lu-Ridge:
The First 50 Years

Compiled and Edited by

Philip A. Brohawn and Craig S. Schenning

Printed in The United States of America

Compiled and edited by Philip Brohawn and Craig Schenning

ISBN-13: 978-0-9841065-2-3

ISBN-10: 0-9841065-2-9

Looking for a publisher?

At Old Line Publishing we are always looking for authors and original manuscripts. We hope that you will contact us and share your thoughts, ideas, stories, and/or already written material with us so that we can help you turn your idea into a timeless treasure and share it with the world.

Old Line Publishing, LLC

P.O. Box 624

Hampstead, MD 21074

Toll-Free Phone: 877-866-8820

Email: oldlinepublishing@comcast.net

Website: www.oldlinepublishingllc.com

Dedication

This book is dedicated to the campers, counselors, staff members, directors, and all those who have walked the hallowed grounds of Mar-Lu-Ridge. Over the last 50 years Mar-Lu-Ridge has touched the lives of thousands of individuals, inspiring some to the ministry of our Lord through pastoral education and moving others to continue the ministry of Mar-Lu-Ridge by volunteering their time and energy to the camp. It is only through the efforts of all of you that the camp has been able to touch the lives of so many people. For 50 years the Holy Spirit has dwelled on this mountain, living and breathing in the hearts and minds of those willing to allow Christ into their lives and manifesting itself in the actions of all those who have shared the Good News of Jesus Christ with others.

Table of Contents

Introduction

Initially, the creation of this book was done for one reason: to create a formal history of the camp from its early beginnings in 1959 to its 50th anniversary in 2009. However, as the researching and writing continued for this book, we knew that it would be more than just a chronological accounting of the camp. It quickly became apparent that for many campers, counselors, and staff members this book would be a long awaited trip down memory lane as many faded and forgotten faces were seen once again amongst the pages of Mar-Lu-Ridge history. For others, this book would be a cherished memento of the time they got lost on the hike, or the cookout that went totally wrong, or the slow recollection of that favorite song that was sung after each meal.

For those who were a part of Mar-Lu-Ridge history, we hope that this book will not stay in your hands. We hope that like the Good News of Christ, you will share your thoughts and memories about Mar-Lu-Ridge with others and that you will use this book to encourage those who have not experienced Christ in the great out-of-doors to go to the Ridge where the opportunity to see, feel and hear God is still present today.

Acknowledgements

We would personally like to recognize the following individuals for their assistance in completing this book. Without their help this treasured book would not be complete: Ilona Ries, Marian Bell, Hermine Saunders, Edna May Merson, John Bassett, Liz Brohawn, Andrew Rickel, Beth Ziegler-Downin, Darrell Layman, Christopher Poling, Vicki Charitonuk-Beilfuss, Karin Lindholm-Belsheim, Ted Meyers, Gary Horne, Sarah Webster-Lefler, Kris Brown, and LaVern Rasmussen.

From the Editor

I am pleased to have had the opportunity to work with Craig Schenning to chronicle this history of Mar-Lu-Ridge. Craig and I endeavored to make this history as accurate and thorough as possible. We compiled information from historical records, input from others, and our own memories.

I was blessed to grow up at Mar-Lu-Ridge. I was there as a child when the first tree was cut on December 31, 1958. I spent the first camping season of 1959 in Cabin #2, and I have lived year-round on the mountain since 1960. It is an interesting realization to know that I am likely the only person who has been at Mar-Lu-Ridge since its beginning.

Philip A. Brohawn

That's not to say that I was a part of all that happened, but I was, at least, an observer. I'm sure that if Berkeley Pearson and Elmer Bartlett (those most responsible for the construction of the buildings here at MLR) were alive today, they would tell you how, as a kid, I followed them around as they were actually constructing these buildings and asked them countless questions. When I was older, I was a counselor, summer staff member, and program director through 1985. In 1986 I took a 12-month job with the school system, but I have continued to live on the mountain with my family the entire time.

This book is a tribute to all those who have helped to make the vision a reality. First, I am proud to have been a part of this project so that I could honor my parents for their more than 30 years of service to Mar-Lu-Ridge. It was their mission. It was their life. It was that simple. It was

that complicated.

Then I remember the 'founding fathers' who have been recognized in the early pages of this book. Their vision and service were critical to making Mar-Lu-Ridge a reality. I remember them with great respect.

There were many full-time staff members over the years who are not mentioned by name in the text but whose contributions to the construction and maintenance of MLR have been invaluable. The cooks here have been such an important part of life here on the Ridge. They always took such great care of us. I fondly remember back in the late 1960s when the counselors brought Patsy out of the kitchen in Lodge #2 to sing "Down by the Old Mill Stream" with all of us on staff! Their names are too numerous to list, but they deserve our thanks. The secretaries who have worked in the office have also played a vital role. Marion Bell, the first MLR secretary, was like a big sister to me for years as I grew up here on the Ridge.

Mar-Lu-Ridge operates year round, but for most of us the memories that are shared are from the summer camping program. Being on summer staff was a life changing experience. While those hundreds of names do not appear within the pages of this book, most of the summer staff pictures are included. If you came to MLR in the summer, I believe that you will look at those pictures, and they will provoke pleasant memories. And, finally, thanks go to all of those who have unselfishly volunteered their service over the past 50 years.

Secretaries/Office Managers

Marion Bell
Mary Wenschoff
Patricia Scott
Helen Sheppard
Cindy Cannon

Maintenance and Construction Personnel

Berkeley Pearson
Elmer Bartlett
Maryland Hale
George Lewis
Kevin Brunk
Pat Main
Edgar Bartlett
Mike Goad
Mike Ryan
Harry Yost
Collin Cole
Jeffrey Mohr
Basil Lewis
Bill Garza

Do You Remember?

"Go Tell It on the Mountain"
S'mores
The "Mar-Lu-Five"
Volleyball Tournaments
Skits Around the Campfire
The Peddler's Grave
Trash Bag Raincoats
The Old Red Truck
Hauling Luggage to the Barn
Thursday Night Dances
Fried Chicken
Cookouts
Friday Night Watermelon
The Walk-ins
The Helipad
Buddy Burners
End of Summer Staff Parties
#10 Tin Cans
Hikes to Area #3
Weddings at the Chapel
Dog Stones
Overnights in the Barn
Johns I and II
Left-Handed Smoke Shifters
The "Aquanuts"
Toad and Turtle Races
The Retreat House
Newcomb
Hiking to Point-of-Rocks
Hiking to the Power Lines
Name Tags

The Camp Store
Bug Juice
NIFDA
"Down by the Old Mill Stream"
Cruisers
Closing Worship Services
Saturday Night "Time-off" for Staff
Swim time
Buzzard Rock
Mar-Lu Postcards
Morning Devotions
"The Ash Grove"
Hobo Dinners
Mock Olympics
The Emergency Bell
Friday Night Campfire/Worship
Muscle Beach
Aggie's Tavern
Three Ponds
Hidden Pond
Ice Candles
Macramé Bracelets
Gimp
Pop-Tart Raids
Nutty Buddies
Directing Traffic
The Caboose
The Green Songbooks
Camp Group Pictures
Four-Square Ball
Gnats, Gnats and more Gnats

The chapel and the cross were first erected on the Ridge in 1961 and since that time they have become two of the most photographed items at Mar-Lu-Ridge. Still today, they are the iconic symbols of what Mar-Lu-Ridge is all about: giving praise and worship to our Lord in the great out-of-doors.

The 1950s

The decade of the 1950s was the genesis of Mar-Lu-Ridge. Talented leaders with vision and drive began with a dream and started to make that dream a reality.

1955

The vision that was to become Mar-Lu-Ridge began in 1955 at the One Hundred Thirty-Sixth Annual Convention of The Evangelical Lutheran Synod of Maryland. As a result, the following action was adopted:

> *"That the Committee on Christian Education be charged to prepare specific plans for the establishment of a Synodical camp and conference center on the territory of the Synod and report to the 1956 Convention."*

And thus, the committee began its work.

1956

The report presented in 1956 by Chairperson Dr. Margaret B. Ballard focused on two major tasks which confronted the Committee. The first of these tasks was to identify the purpose, principles and program for

Located amongst hickories, oaks, and maples this spectacular grove of beech trees is similar to those found on the ridge that separates the Middletown and Frederick Valleys: a ridge soon to be home to a new Christian camp.

church camping that would be sponsored by the Synod. Research into church camping was conducted and recommendations were made that the program should operate year-round, include a summer camp with programs for youth through adults, as well as family camping, and provide all the necessary resources for small group camping experiences.

Further recommendations stated that the site selected should have an acreage of one acre per camper, so that the site should be at least 200-250 acres in size and that the Synod should take title of the property.

The second task was to investigate available sites. Sites investigated included a farm property west of Clear Spring, Maryland; a farm near Smithsburg, Maryland; several properties near Hagerstown, Maryland; the K-B Ranch near Thurmont, Maryland; property in Largent, West Virginia; and a river-side property near the Cacapon State Park close to Berkeley Springs, West Virginia.

View of Autumn foliage in the wooded mountain area of Jefferson, Maryland.

1957

An additional site was considered in 1957. A parcel of wooded mountain land between Doubs, Maryland and Jefferson, Maryland was visited by members from the Maryland Synod Executive Board, the Committee on Parish Education, and consultants of the Parish School Board of the ULCA. All agreed, for the first time, that the Jefferson site should be the location of the new church camp. By unanimous action, the Executive Board appointed a subcommittee to initiate negotiations to acquire parcels of land owned by different persons.

The property was described as an unimproved, mostly wooded area, on a ridge overlooking the Middletown and Frederick Valleys. A Study Conference, attended by leaders from our own Church and the National Council of Churches, was held on April 11th in Baltimore to prepare for the most effective use of the campsite once the land has been acquired.

This early undated photo, taken in front of Salem-on-the-Mountain Chapel, shows many individuals who played a vital role in the creation and organization of Mar-Lu-Ridge. From left to right; Rev. Roland Ries, Rev. Harry Krug, Bishop Paul Orso, Mrs. Ruth Brohawn, Mr. Philip Brohawn, unknown gentleman, Rev, L. David Bollinger and Howard White.

Rev. Harry V. Krug was one of the early leaders of the camp and a strong proponent of the Salem-on-the-Mountain Chapel. (Photo courtesy of Carroll Lutheran Village)

Rev. Michael Kretsinger, served as chairman of the Program Development Committee. (Photo courtesy of Julia Kretsinger).

1958

A sub-committee of the Parish Education Committee of the Synod, the Camping Committee, was developed and composed of the following members: Miss Edna May Merson, Dr. Warren Evans, and Pastors Russell Fink, Michael Kretsinger, Harry Krug, Roland Ries, and L. David Bollinger, Chair. These members familiarized themselves with camp philosophy and newer trends in church camping.

Over 290 acres of land were purchased and surveyed. The Camp Committee selected W. Glenn Wallace, a nationally known camp architect, as the camp architect. Mr. Wallace and the Committee walked the property on March 8th, and Mr. Wallace was "favorably impressed with the site." The Camp Committee considered the possibilities of providing areas on site for camping, conference groups, picnicking, swimming, and parking.

The Committee divided into two sub-committees. The Rev. Harry Krug chaired one on the development of physical facilities. The Rev. Michael Kretsinger chaired the subcommittee on program development.

In December of 1958, Mr. Philip J. Brohawn was hired on a part-time basis as coordinator of development and supervisor of construction. An active member of St. Mark's Lutheran Church in Hampstead, Mr. Brohawn had a background in engineering and construction.

In preparation for camping for the summer of 1959, the Committee planned the following building program: one lodge (Dining Hall/Lodge #1), which would be equipped with a dining room, capable of seating 90 persons, a kitchen, toilet facilities to accommodate 42 campers, and an administration room; four winterized cabins (Cabins #1 - #4, although Cabin #3 would not be built until 1960); and 12 hogan shelters.

On December 31, 1958 a special ceremony took place at what is now the beginning of the road to Mar-Lu-Ridge. At that time the entire mountain was covered with trees. One tree was cut down on the last day of 1958 to inaugurate the ambitious construction plan that was to continue for more than a decade.

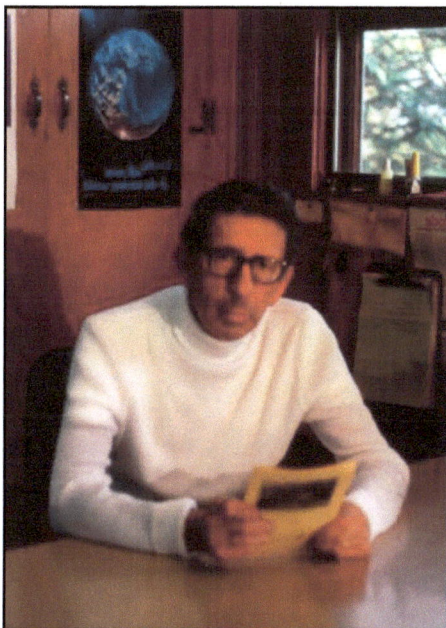

Mr. Philip J. Brohawn was the first Manager/ Director. His vision and leadership were crucial to the development of the camp and its philosophy of small group co-educational camping.

Mrs. Ruth Brohawn worked side by side with her husband for over 33 years during which she was Registrar and Associate Manager/Director.

Early, but undated photo of the camp road prior to its paving later in the 1960s.

Besides lodging, one of the first things erected on the camp was this telephone booth that connected campers and staff to the outside world.

1959

The first task to be completed was the camp road. This was no easy feat as trees and rocks had to be removed through two miles of wooded, mountainous terrain. Fifty years later you can still see many of the large stones that were moved in 1959.

When the road reached the site where Lodge #1 was to be built, a telephone booth was erected next to the site. Campers and volunteers from the early years remember this phone booth. In those days prior to cell phones, it was the connection to the outside world. While the mountain was not exactly a wilderness in 1959, it was clearly more remote and isolated than it is now. Looking across the valley, one saw very few houses.

The four lane highway that is now Route 340 didn't exist at that time. Route 340 was a single lane road that ran through the middle of Jefferson. And, on the east side of the mountain, the highway that is currently Route 15 did not exist. Route 15 ran through Buckeystown and east of Adamstown, several miles further away than its present location.

Lodge #1 was constructed as well as three cabins – those currently numbered 1, 2 and 4. The glass in the front of the lodge, as well as the deck surrounding it, allowed campers to see a stunning view including three states!

The Synod Camp and Conference Center opened its camping ministry and the site was dedicated in June of 1959.

Initial camper registration had been limited to 5 campers from each parish during the first month and then on a first-come, first-served basis. Six one-week camp periods were scheduled along with one week of family camp. The Rev. Albert Burkhardt was selected as the first Registrar.

Camps that first summer included: two Junior camps with a total of 83 campers; two Junior-High camps with 69 campers; one Senior-High camp with 17 campers; and one family camp with nine families. Including the 36 leaders, there were a total of 247 campers and leaders for that first summer.

After Labor Day there was immediate use of the lodge and cabins for retreats. Many church

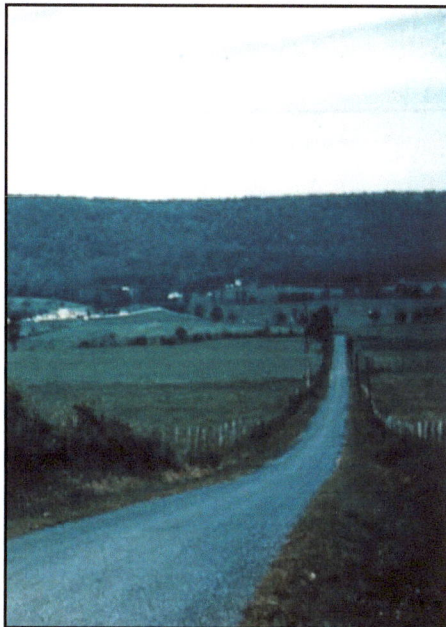

Early, but undated photo of Lander Road, taken near the present site of the Shell Station.

Photo from the Dedication of Mar-Lu-Ridge in June of 1959. This stage area was set up across the road from Lodge 1.

"I have fond memories of the summer of 1959. What an adventure it was for me to spend 2 months living in the mountains! I was 11 years old. I lived in Cabin# 2 with my Mom and Dad. How exciting it was to be part of this great new adventure! I was also a junior camper that first summer, and I slept in a hogan across from Lodge #1. I still remember some of the campers who were in my group ."

Philip A. Brohawn

The dedication ceremony as viewed from the porch of Lodge #1 in June of 1959.

An early, but undated photo, showing the completion of Cabin #2. This photo was most likely taken during the summer of 1959.

While no formal numbers have been found, it appears as though hundreds of supporters gathered for the dedication ceremony presented in June of 1959. A closer inspection of the picture reveals the hogans that were the first living quarters for summer campers of that year.

groups had to be turned down due to lack of space. Demand for use made development of a complete facility for Synod-wide uses a rational decision. More construction was planned.

Before the end of 1959, construction began on another cabin, a camp manager's residence, a picnic shelter, and a shop/garage for maintenance and storage.

The Camp Committee consisted of: Pastor Michael Kretsinger, Chairperson; Pastor Harry Krug, Chairperson of Subcommittee on Building and Development; Pastor Thomas Sinn, Chairperson of Subcommittee on Program Development; Mr. Howard White; Mr. Marcellus Bacon; Miss Virginia Sorensen; Pastor Barron Maberry; Pastor Lloyd Seiler; Pastor John McGuigan; Mr. Earl Yingling; and ex officio – Director of Parish Education, Chairperson of Parish Education Committee, Camp Registrar Pastor Albert Burkhardt, and Camp Treasurer, Mr. Meredith Mackley.

This undated photo of Lodge 1 was most likely taken shortly after its completion in the summer of 1959.

The 1960s

The 1960s was a decade of incredible growth at Mar-Lu-Ridge both in terms of physical facilities and in numbers of campers and retreat groups who used the site.

1960

Mar-Lu-Ridge became the official name of the Synod's camp and conference center. The facility's name represented both **Mar**yland **Lu**theran and **Mar**tin **Lu**ther on the **Ridge**.

Synod small-group camp leaders were trained who became the envy of many church camping groups. Mr. Philip J. Brohawn assumed "directorship" of the facility and matters of information, bookings, registration, leadership recruitment, training, and scheduling of Mar-Lu-Ridge could all now be done from one location. The director's residence was completed and Mr. Brohawn and his wife, Ruth, and sons, Lee and Philip, moved to Mar-Lu-Ridge in June.

The fourth cabin (the present day Cabin #3), a double-decker, was completed in February. The shop and picnic pavilion were also completed (this picnic pavilion is the one that is on the right side of the road across from the shop). Construction also commenced on the second of four planned dining halls – Lodge/Dining Hall #2. One pond was constructed at the bottom of the mountain with a second, larger one under-

This photo taken in December of 1960 shows a newly completed Cabin #6. This cabin was just one of eleven cabins that would be built between Area #1 and Area #2.

Finding an adequate water supply was a major issue. Several wells were drilled on top of the mountain that were over 600 feet deep. Even at this depth little or no water was found. So several wells were drilled at the base of the mountain (near the site of the ponds). These wells pumped the water halfway up the mountainside into a holding tank buried in the ground. From this tank another pump moved the water to a holding tank buried at the highest location on top of the mountain – directly across the road from the present day location of the chapel. A steep, winding, unpaved trail that started by the shop accessed these wells. Many scary, but exciting trips were made up and down this trail in the camp's four wheel drive truck to keep this system operating!

way. This was one of the major hiking destinations in the early years.

The need for a swimming pool was emphasized. During the first years of the summer program, campers rode a school bus from Mar-Lu-Ridge to the Braddock Heights swimming pool twice a week. These trips were lots of fun as campers sang camp songs throughout the entire ride!

Though not on the Master Plan, a chapel found its way onto the committee's planning. Construction started for more cabins in what was to become known as

Area #2. Additional power and water lines were constructed. Trails and fire breaks were cleared into the mountainside.

Attendance doubled in all aspects of usage. Plans were made for additional expansion. There were 357 campers representing 97 congregations for the summer camp program which was moved from the general conference area thus enabling the site to carry on conferencing and camping simultaneously during the summer months. Seventy trained leaders assisted with the summer program and 2,623 retreat participants were in attendance during the year.

.1961

The name MAR-LU-RIDGE was now carved deep in the hearts of hundreds of boys and girls, men and women and was known far beyond the borders of the Maryland Synod as the name of an outstanding Christian Camp and Conference Center.

As given in the report of the Convention, "The Mar-Lu-Ridge environ-

This photo taken in February of 1961 shows the construction of Dining Hall/Lodge #2. This was the second of four dining halls or lodges that would be built on the Ridge.

ment, facilities, and programs are fulfilling the great need of boys and girls for the best in Christian guidance, and their responsiveness to fun, challenge, and understanding the Christian way of life."

More congregations were using the facility. The elevated topography of Mar-Lu-Ridge did much to orient the mind and heart of the Christian. It provided a place "high and lifted up" and made it easy for visitors to the Ridge to realize the temple experience of Isaiah. As the Psalmist says, "He will set me high upon the rock. And now my head shall be lifted up... I will sing and make melody to the Lord."

Some 531 summer campers represented 111 congregations. Camping for blind and deaf participants started that year. The interaction between these campers and the regular session campers was a wonderful experience for both.

1962

Two very important construction projects were completed and became available for use this year. Salem-On-The-Mountain Chapel and the swimming pool were completed thanks to the continued donations of many individuals and congregations.

Salem-On-The-Mountain was named for Salem Lutheran from Baltimore, whose congregation donated $15,000 toward its construction. Dedication of the Chapel was held on June 2 when over 1,500 people visited that day and attended the three dedication worship celebrations. The A-frame chapel with the front wall of glass looked over the beauty of God's creation across the Maryland landscape of the Middletown Valley, over the Potomac River into Virginia, and through the gap at Harper's Ferry into West Virginia.

The new swimming pool was a big hit with campers and staff alike. The excited voices of happy campers could be heard from quite a distance!

Ten new hogans were constructed to enhance the pioneer camping experience. Five hundred and eighty-eight summer campers represented 107 congregations.

This photo, taken in the fall of 1961, shows the supporting trusses and beams giving shape to the chapel, a shape that has been a focal point of many pictures at Mar-Lu-Ridge.

This photo, actually taken in the summer of 1979, shows a completed chapel with a similar view.

This image of the chapel was taken soon after its completion in the summer of 1962. This image, as well as a number of similar images, has become symbolic of Mar-Lu-Ridge and has been used on post cards, pamphlets, brochures, and many other items.

This photo from June of 1962 shows the newly completed pool located in Area #2.

The business ability and knowledge of architecture and construction of Philip Brohawn was "invaluable to the physical development of Mar-Lu -Ridge." Facilities were said to be ahead of their time. At this time these facilities included 2 dining lodges, 9 completely furnished cabins, a staff cabin, chapel, swimming pool, picnic pavilion, manager's residence, and 22 hogans.

Early indication was that Mar-Lu-Ridge was one of the most significant developments in the life of the Maryland Synod in this generation. "Its opportunity for individual spiritual growth, for Christian education, for evangelism, for Christian community, and for the teaching of real Christian stewardship started to be realized. The potential was great." In only 4 years, there was unbelievable growth.

1963

The biggest story of 1963 was the February 3rd purchase of the Talbert Farm located on Mountville Road immediately at the end of the camp road. This property (to be named Area #3) included additional acreage and a farmhouse, a tractor barn, and a bank barn. Work began on remodeling the farmhouse into a completely self-contained retreat house. Work on the former tractor barn started with the goal of refurbishing it into a two-level dining/sleeping/retreat facility (Lodge #3).

Small group living groups for summer campers were planned and 16 arks were constructed for use in these four small group areas. Arks had replaced the previously used canvas covered hogans. The wooden arks were sturdier and windows made them brighter.

An entirely new water system was developed for Area #3 and a pond containing almost a million gallons of water was built.

Two-thirds of the Maryland Synod's congregations were represented in the summer camping program with 768 campers. There were over 7,000 retreat participants, which was almost a 60% increase.

1964

According to camp authorities outside of the Synod "who are acquainted with all the Lutheran camps and conference centers," Mar-Lu-Ridge, "stands at the head of the class when all Lutheran camps are called into session." Purpose, philosophy, basic principles, program along with qualified personnel, and the well-planned facilities of Mar-Lu-Ridge made it second to none. Mar-Lu-Ridge was included in national publications as that which stood above all other Lutheran facilities. The philosophy and objectives set forth in the new national LCA manual on Church Camping published that year did not differ at all from those drawn up by the Maryland Camp and Conference Committee in the late-fifties.

Area #3 (or the Junior Camp Area) was officially opened in the Summer of 1964 and it accommodated nearly 500 junior campers (grades 4-6). Although not physically complete, Area #3 offered a camping experience for junior campers that was similar in many ways to that of the junior high campers in Areas #1 and #2. The terms "up-the-hill" and "down-the-hill" came into use as campers, staff, and materials moved between

This photo taken in the summer of 1964 shows the barn and parking area in Area #3. After children were dropped off on Sunday, this parking area became a great place for group games and camp activities.

This image, taken in the summer of 1964, shows the newly renovated Lodge #3 as seen from the Retreat House porch.

This undated photo shows the construction of the pond in Area #3. When the pond was completed, it contained nearly 1,000,000 gallons of water.

Although taken from a different angle, this photo from July of 1968 shows the completed pond in Area #3. The pond area had several adjacent group areas as well as a campfire circle.

This undated photo shows the tractor barn in Area #3. The shell of this structure was used to create the new Lodge #3.

This undated photo shows the completion of Lodge #3, circa 1964.

camp areas. For the first time, there were over 1000 campers with 1,125 in attendance at the 23 camping sessions and representing 133 congregations.

Junior campers rode from Area 3 to the swimming pool at the top of the mountain in a wagon pulled behind the camp truck. The children loved this experience. Several years later a second swimming pool was built in Area #3.

Ruth Brohawn, now the camp registrar, reported that as of March 10 of that year, all sessions except three were filled. This meant that all youth who wanted to attend were unable to do so. Campers who did not register in time were placed on waiting lists.

For the first time, and only five years after the camp opened, more than 10,000 people of all ages visited Mar-Lu-Ridge.

Other accomplishments for the year included a remodeling of the Retreat House which was completed in early June and for the first time, plans for a high comfort retreat facility, Mar-Lu-Tel, also known as Area #4, became public.

This early undated image shows the campers from the Area #3 being towed to Area #2 for swim time. The pool in Area #3 had not yet been constructed.

This photo from the spring of 1959 shows the earliest construction of the two mile-long camp road. The road would eventually be paved in the years from 1964 - 1966.

I was privileged to serve as a Summer Staff leader at Mar-Lu-Ridge from 1962 to 1973. I experienced much of the early foundation of my spiritual journey & faith life that has guided me throughout these years from having been a part of the Mar-Lu mountain ministry. As a leader I was also in a teaching role, and one never knows for sure how far & wide one's influence stretches. I feel that I learned more from campers than I could ever have taught them. Working with primarily Junior age campers, who were always ready to learn & experience God's outdoor creation was a "real joy." I also had the honor & privilege of working with camps for the blind, deaf, & inner city, which enriched my life tremendously.

Dave "Hip-Hip" Miller

Four thousand feet of the dusty, gravel camp road were surfaced. The area that was surfaced included the part of the road where all of the buildings were located.

1965

Two more double-decker cabins were constructed on the Ridge thus increasing sleeping capacity while also providing meeting space as the upstairs of each was designed for that purpose.

There were 1,313 summer campers with over 300 leaders

assisting. There were 9,566 visitors just for retreats alone.

Maintaining an adequate water supply became a major concern as over one million gallons of water were used just during summer camp.

1966

Work started in February on the construction of a new 55,000-gallon covered reservoir. This reservoir is situated at the high point of the mountain directly across from the Chapel. In later years, a pavilion was built on top of it. An additional well was also drilled.

Two additional ponds (making it into the Three Ponds area) were created and the asphalt surfacing of the entire camp road was completed, much to the delight of those who traveled it regularly!

While the camping program continued to focus on small group camping a new camp was added to the summer schedule. A Camp for Special Youth was initiated and had over 30 campers in attendance.

This photo shows the construction of the 55,000 gallon water reservoir built in 1966. The reservoir was located underneath the pavilion across from Salem-on-the-Mountain.

While not the snowstorm mentioned below, this image from February of 1972 shows a similar scenario where several feet of snow lay on the ground. Camp personnel were responsible for clearing camp roads during the winter and making it accessible, especially for emergency vehicles.

A ferocious snowstorm blanketed Mar-Lu-Ridge during the winter of 1966. In late January more than a foot of new snow fell on top of a foot of already existing snow, and was then followed by 60 – 70 mph winds. To this day, I have never seen more snow piled so high! Frederick County Public Schools were closed for 8 and 1/2 days during a ten day period! MLR's white four wheel drive truck with snow plow attached was literally buried in snow on the camp road in front of the shop. The only thing that could be seen of the truck was the searchlight mounted on top of the cab!

With no way to dig out, we had to wait for help. Sitting in the living room of the manager/director's residence, we could look into the valley below and see a large road grader with a huge V-blade slowly making its way along Fry Road at the base of the mountain. The road grader was used because regular snow removal trucks could not move through the huge drifts. The road grader crawled at a snail's pace, and then, after dark, it would stop completely, and soon after, there were intense flashes of bright lights. These flashes were from welding torches repairing the broken blade and its supports as it was battered trying to move so much snow! This scene repeated itself at least four times within the distance of half mile. From the night we observed this until that road grader made it to the camp office, a distance of about four miles, it was a day and half later!

Philip A. Brohawn

Mar-Lu-Ridge was in use for 242 days of the year and continued to be regarded as the premier Lutheran camp facility. However, priorities began to shift from new construction to maintenance.

1967

Construction started on Mar-Lu-Tel, also referred to as Dining Hall #4, Lodge #4 and/or Unit #4. This building was the last of the four units on the original Master Site Plan. Original plans said that Unit #4 would consist of 5 buildings all joined by breezeways.

Mar-Lu-Ridge received a bequest from the will of Mr. Harry E. Schmidt of Salem Lutheran, Baltimore, for the development of a wildlife exhibit and nature center. The live exhibit consisted of a buck and two does (contributed by the State of Maryland and the National Park Service) as well as a pair of raccoons and one deodorized skunk.

The first camp for inner city youth was very successful and was directed by The Rev. Donald Keyser.

Besides deer, additional inhabitants of the wild-life pen included both domesticated and wild geese as seen in this early photo.

To date, this is the only known image of the deodorized skunk, one of the first inhabitants of the wildlife exhibit along the camp road.

This February 1967 photo shows the construction of the first phase of the new Mar-Lu-Tel Conference Center located on the hill overlooking Area #3.

The camp was involved in outdoor education programs with both Montgomery and Frederick County School systems. There were 276 days of facility use for 10,448 people.

1968

This year was the time to celebrate what has been accomplished in 10 years. As reported by The Rev. Harry Krug, "…the lean years…the discouragements, doubts, and fears of those B. C. (before camp) years. The efforts, determination and struggle of the committee bore fruit and the mountain became alive." He also revealed that on the second day of camp in 1959, the only well went dry – another well had to be dug.

Mr. Philip Brohawn continued to receive high praises for his leadership and the direction that Mar-Lu-Ridge had taken.

There were 1,428 campers for summer camp, which represented capacity usage of the facilities. A total of 142 inner city youth also attended. Almost 11,000 participants were in attendance for retreats with use of facility for 320 days accommodating as many as seven groups on a given day.

Construction projects for the year included the completion of the first section of Unit 4 (to be named the Mar-Lu-Ridge Conference Center), the outdoor worship centers for both Area 2 and 3, and an activity shelter for Areas 1 & 2 (pavilion across from Chapel). All cabin interiors and exteriors were repainted.

During a turbulent year in which both Dr. Martin Luther King and Bobby Kennedy were assassinated, Mar-Lu-Ridge remained an oasis of peace and Christian fellowship.

1969

Mar-Lu-Ridge was in use for 340 days during the year! In addition to church related activities, 38 weeks of outdoor education for Frederick and Montgomery County Public Schools were held at Mar-Lu-Ridge.

The construction of the new Conference Center continued. Plans for the Center had been modified from five to three interconnected buildings.

This photo taken during the summer of 1968 shows the construction of phases two and three of the Conference Center.

The 1970s

The era of construction came to a close in the 1970s. Summer camping remained popular, and many retreat groups continued to use the Mar-Lu-Ridge facilities.

1970

The written report to the 1970 Convention thanked Phil and Ruth Brohawn by saying, "As we begin our 12th year on the Mountain, we salute the Manager-Director of Mar-Lu-Ridge, Mr. Philip Brohawn and his good wife. A better pair to develop, guide, and operate a camp and conference center you'll never see."

The construction of the final phase of Unit #4, the Conference and Retreat Center (Mar-Lu-Tel), occurred this year. The modern looking building with a front wall of glass and a huge deck overlooking the panoramic Frederick Valley to the east, consisted of three buildings, all connected, with individual sleeping rooms and bathrooms.

This year marked a major milestone. All construction detailed in the original Master Site Plan had been completed! This was a time of much celebration. Mar-Lu-Ridge was operating at a high level of usage and expectations were high!

This photo shows the completed Conference Center that sits overlooking Area #3.

This 1978 photo shows a helicopter landing on the helipad which was constructed in 1971.
The helipad was removed 30 years later.

1971

John Bassett was named Assistant to the Manager/Director. John had already served the camp as counselor for five years. He would serve Mar-Lu-Ridge for the next 26 years!

In order to assure the safety of potentially snowbound retreat groups, power lines and trees were moved to build a helipad with an unobstructed approach. It was quite a sight to see a helicopter landing on the Ridge! The helipad was eventually dismantled in 2001 in order to provide more level space for outdoor activities.

1972

Mrs. Ruth Brohawn assumed the title of Associate Manager/ Director. In addition to doing the registration for summer camps, she was also responsible for food service at all three lodges.

Over 1,000 girls and boys registered for the summer programs while 12,700 other youth and adults attended various functions at Mar-Lu-Ridge throughout the year. MLR facilities were in use for 334 days.

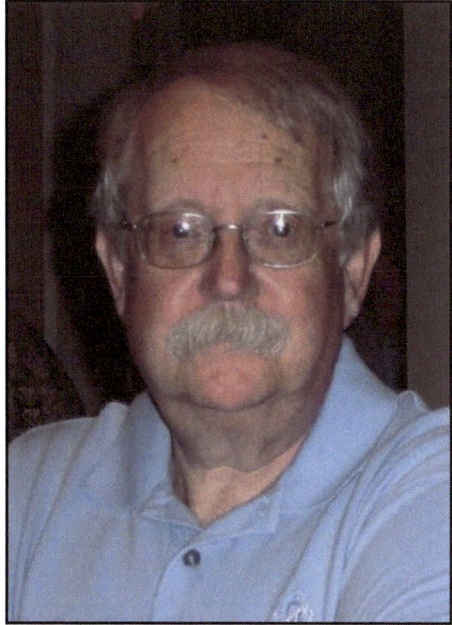

For over 30 years John Bassett served Mar-Lu-Ridge in a wide variety of positions including Assistant to the Manager/Director.

During June of 1972, Hurricane Agnes dropped huge amounts of rainfall along the East Coast of the U.S. resulting in widespread flooding. We were glad to be on a mountaintop and felt somewhat relieved to have the campers living in arks! However, even on a mountaintop, the hurricane had its effects. Needless to say, there were many indoor activities that week. But, more significantly, the excessive rainfall caused the pond in Area #3 to rise to the level that groups 4 and 5 would be cut-off and unable to get back to Lodge 3. So these campers were evacuated and spent the night at the Conference Center or Retreat House– high, dry, and safe!

1973

Phil and Ruth Brohawn were officially thanked for 15 years of service with a celebration held on October 14th in the Salem-On-The-Mountain Chapel, followed by dinner in the Conference Center. The following appeared on the back of the program for that celebration. "This man, who was called as Manager-Director of Mar-Lu-Ridge in the summer of 1959, proved to be the Joshua to lead us into the Promised Land. With his leadership, the 'land-locked' tract of land in the Catoctin Mountains was soon to be liberated." The next quote was written in the 1973 Report to the Synod Convention. "In fifteen years the Conference and Retreat Center of Mar-Lu-Ridge has grown from infancy to maturity." The report stated, "MISSION ACCOMPLISHED."

This was the last year of the Camp Committee as a separate entity.

Over 920 campers attended the summer programs which were still primarily focused on the general small group camping experience. Approximately 13,000 people used the facility throughout the year.

This photo from the summer of 1975 shows a group of canoe campers getting ready for one of their river adventures.

This undated photo shows the building of one of the "arks." These arks were more permanent, sturdier, and brighter than their predecessor, the "hogan."

1974

Two new programs were initiated for the 1974 summer camping season - Canoe Camp and Appalachian Trail Hiking. Canoe campers ventured to nearby scenic waterways including the Potomac, Shenandoah, and Monocacy Rivers. Trail hikers were driven to the nearby Appalachian Trail and spent several days hiking and carrying all of their food and supplies along the historic, mountainous trail.

1975

Another new summer program was advertised in the 1975 summer camping brochure – Bicycle Camp. Campers took multiple-day trips and visited scenic and historic sites. It was exceptionally hot that year during bicycle camp, and that pattern continued for several years. It seemed that bicycle camp was destined to happen during the hottest week of the summer! For the year, there were over 950 summer campers and nearly

11,300 retreat participants.

1976

The age-groupings of the campers were changed to align with the middle school concept of the public schools. Junior camp, previously for fourth, fifth, and sixth graders, was changed to third, fourth, and fifth graders. Junior High camp was opened to those campers who had completed sixth grade.

Mar-Lu-Ridge always sought scholarship funding for needy campers. However, finding these scholarships became a more difficult task in the mid-1970s. Getting enough volunteers to work during the summer was also a challenge.

1977

In early March, Mar-Lu-Ridge hosted the national Tri Lutheran Camp Directors Conference. Over 120 camp directors from all over the United States and Canada had the opportunity to visit Mar-Lu-Ridge, to see what had been accomplished, and to enjoy the three-state view across the valley to the west.

For the first time, Mar-Lu-Ridge offered a two-week Junior High Cabin Camp which was attended by 39 youth and overall there was an 11% increase in summer camper attendance over the previous year.

Since alignment with the middle school concept had opened Junior Camp to younger campers, MLR developed a new living area closer to Lodge 3 for the youngest of these to make them feel more secure. The new group, composed of four new arks, became the fifth small group in Area #3. That camping area could now accommodate at least 70 campers per week. Many readers of this book have fond memories of sitting by a blazing campfire overlooking the pond in the junior camping area.

1978

The cost of living had increased significantly and the need to raise camper fees became an issue. Camper fees never generated a profit, but it was necessary to raise them in order to prevent losing money.

Summer camping remained popular as Mar-Lu-Ridge operated at almost total capacity with 1023 summer campers.

1979

Horseback Riding Camp was a new program for the summer of 1979. The horses and instructors for the budding equestrians were provided by a local stable.

Maintenance was becoming a concern as most of the facilities at Mar-Lu-Ridge were approaching 20 years of age. The buildings would soon require major renovation such as replacing shingles, floor tile, furnaces, etc.

In March, the Finance and Budget Committee suggested and the Executive Board requested a ten-year projection of the maintenance needs at Mar-Lu-Ridge. The Synod Convention unanimously approved

This photo taken during the summer of 1979 shows the first horseback camp. Instruction on riding and animal care was provided by a local stable.

This beautiful "sign-of-the-times" was painted at the bottom of the pool in Area #2 at the beginning of the summer of 1972.

the fund raising appeal for this purpose in the amount of $350,000.

In September, the Executive Board appointed the Mar-Lu-Ridge Committee of the Executive Board as the liaison between the Board and Mar-Lu-Ridge. The chairman of this committee was Pastor Bernard Coates. One of the first decisions made was to implement an important fundraising effort. The committee initiated the 20/20 Appeal. Mar-Lu-Ridge had existed for 20 years, and the committee wanted to assure its success for the next 20 years!

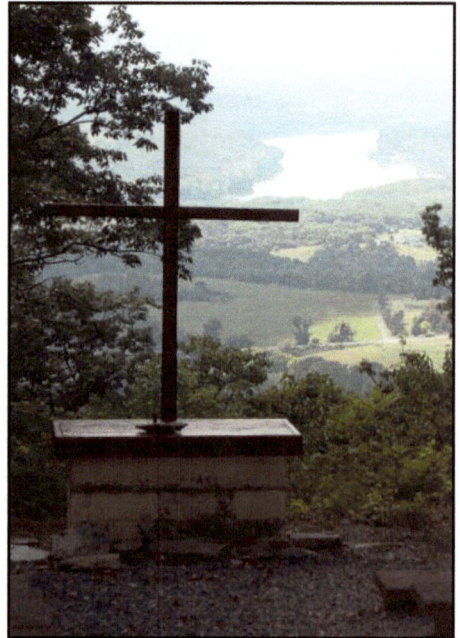

As MLR entered the 1980s, it continued to be a source of inspiration, hope and guidance for many campers, counselors and staff.

The 1980s

During the 1980s, summer camping and retreat groups continued to use Mar-Lu-Ridge as it focused on maintenance and refurbishment of facilities.

1980

The 20/20 Appeal was well underway. A ten-year plan for maintaining and refurbishing the Mar-Lu-Ridge facilities was developed and initiated as the 20/20 funds arrived. There were 1061 summer campers.

1981-1983

By March 5, 1981, the camp had received written pledges of $205,304 through the 20/20 Appeal. With the exception of six financially strapped congregations, all Synod congregations pledged to give. By 1982 pledges had increased to $228,291.

Maintenance and refurbishment projects realized through these funds included painting of all arks in Areas 2 & 3, shower rooms in Area 3, Cabins 1 – 11 inside and out, Lodges 1 - 3, the barn; an addition to the office; new filtration systems in both swimming pools; three freezers and one refrigerator in the lodges; new tables for Lodge #4; new water heaters; new bunks and mattresses; and new tile in some of the cabins.

1983 ... A year of the continued Cold War, "Reganomics", Yuppies, big hair worn with shoulder pads and Mar-Lu-Ridge! MLR was bursting at the seams with campers and we were two college-aged counselors. Every week was filled with new campers with new activities (Canoe! Bike! Two-Week Cabin Camp!) and we enjoyed each new challenge to minister to our awesome campers. But twenty-four hours each weekend was free to hang out with other counselors. We talked, laughed, joked, debated, prayed and became a community of Believers who lived as young followers of Christ. Friendships made during those summers have been life-long. Some friendships (like ours) blossomed into love and marriage. After 23 years of marriage and seeing our son on summer staff, we can say with conviction, "God has blessed Mar-Lu-Ridge and works mightily in the lives of all who seek Him there."

Nancy Hoffmeister Wymer: Camper '77-'79, Counselor '80-'84

Fred Wymer: Camper '73-'82, Counselor '83-'85

1984

This year marked the 25th anniversary of Mar-Lu-Ridge. On September 9, 1984, this milestone was observed with a Service of Celebration and Rededication in the Salem-on-the-Mountain Chapel attended by 200 people. The invitation to the celebration began with the words – "We gather to thank Almighty God for his constant supply of people, money, vision, energy, and ministry opportunities for this community we call Mar-Lu-Ridge."

Lee Brohawn, elder son of Philip and Ruth Brohawn, was hired as Assistant Director, and began taking on responsibilities at Mar-Lu-Ridge. Lee had served as a camp counselor during the early years of Mar-Lu-Ridge and was happy to return full-time. He served in this role for nine years.

The 20/20 Appeal and implementation of the 10-year plan continued on schedule. Nearly 8,500 people used the facilities.

1985

In order to bolster enrollment in the summer camping program the program was opened to even younger campers as Junior Camp accepted youth who had completed second grade.

Additions to the facilities in 1985 included the construction of a bathhouse in lower camping section of Area #2 (which saved many campers and counselors a long hike up the hill!) Prior to the completion of the bathhouse in Area #2 there were only toilets available for use and the structures were seriously dilapidated.

Lee Brohawn served as a camp counselor and later as Assistant Director from 1984– 1993.

The destruction of the "johns down under" as they were known by many, gave way to a more modern bathhouse which included showers as well as sinks and toilets.

This year also saw the installation of an elevator in Lodge #4. The elevator was funded through donations given by the late Fred Gross, a long time and dedicated summer staff member.

Phil and Ruth Brohawn were recognized for 25 years of service to Mar-Lu-Ridge.

1986

Philip A. Brohawn, who had been the summer camping Program Director since 1970, accepted a twelve month position with Frederick County Public Schools precluding him from continuing to work at Mar-Lu-Ridge in the summers. He had been assisting with the Mar-Lu-Ridge summer camping program in various capacities for 24 years.

1987

1987 was a year of transition for Mar-Lu-Ridge. With encouragement from the Commission for a New Lutheran Church, and upon the recommendation of the Transition Team of the Maryland Synod, Evangelical Lutheran Church in America, the formation of the Mar-Lu-Ridge Corporation was approved by the Executive Board in the Spring of 1987.

On June 22, 1987, the Corporation was formed and Philip Brohawn was elected Executive Administrator. It was at the spring meeting of the Executive Board when action was officially taken to form the Corporation. The Articles of Incorporation and Bylaws were adopted, and the property transferred to the Corporation.

A temporary Board of Directors was elected consisting of Bishop Morris Zumbrun, Jack Merriman, and Thomas Markuskewski. At the first meeting of this Board, the following officers of the Corporation were elected: President, Morris Zumbrun; Secretary/Treasurer, Albert Burkhardt; Executive Administrator, Philip J. Brohawn. An advisory Committee was also elected with the following members: The Rev. Darrell Layman, The Rev. George Tuttle, Lois Giles, Marjorie Koch, Kimberly Bond, and David J. Ernat.

1988

For many years both Montgomery and Frederick County Public Schools had been using Mar-Lu-Ridge during the school year for their outdoor education programs. In 1988 both decided to discontinue using Mar-Lu-Ridge and relocated their programs to other sites. This was a significant loss in facility usage.

1989

Thirty years of outdoor ministry at Mar-Lu-Ridge were celebrated on October 1, 1989. "Mar-Lu-Ridge 30th Anniversary on the Mountain … Remembrance and Renewal" was the theme of that celebration. The

As Mar-Lu-Ridge entered the 1990s, the camp continued to be an integral part in the lives of many campers. Campers would return year after year in order to reconnect with both God and friends.

following very appropriate words are from the Prayer of Renewal from that service. "How beautiful is the world around us, how good it is to be here, Lord. All who have come to the Ridge have left as different people. We thank you for this place; for years of dedicated planners and leaders; for those who have supported this center with gifts of love; for the programs and experiences; for the spiritual growth and the warm friendships formed; for new revelations of your love."

This monument located across the road from Lodge #1 was erected to recognize the many gifts and donations given to the camp over the years.

Mar-Lu-Ridge "Holding Fast to What is Good" (1Thess. 5:21)

I attended MLR as a youth and after helping with a church retreat at MLR in the fall of 1973 thought I might apply to be on the summer staff, as I had just been hired as a teacher fresh out of college in Carroll County, Maryland. At that point, I am sure I did not dream I would be on the full-time summer staff for the next 24 years and then a volunteer for 11 years thereafter! If I were to list highs and lows it might look like this:

LOWS: Gnats, sometimes, but I did learn to hold one hand up high. The gnats really do fly to the highest point ,but your arm sort of falls asleep.

HIGHS: (in random order)

1. Met my future wife, Lois, during staff training week of 1974

2. Had the privilege of knowing people like Mr. & Mrs. B.

3. Met, worked, and worshipped with many wonderful people including leaders from other countries including Mr. Yutaka, Mr. Dave, Mr. Robbie, and Miss Nikki to name a few.

4. Pastor Fred

5. John Bassett

6. Elmer, the camp dog faithful and true

7. The campers, of course

8. The freedom to design and carry out different camp weeks like History week, Servant week, Washington DC week, Annapolis week and even MLR goes to Europe Camp along with Lee and Barbara Brohawn.

9. Worship, especially the early Christian worship service where we worshiped in hiding at first, but then left with joy to spread the Word.

10. Seeing former campers come back as leaders and getting to work with them.

11. Did I mention Lois???

12. Campfires, Bible studies, and picnic tables

13. All the time singing and Friday night worship

14. The wonderful cooks

15. I love the mountains and Mar-Lu-Ridge

Finally, I once heard a preacher say it's the angels who are most jealous of us below. Sure they have neat wings and get to fly about and they sing real good, but they miss out on the greatest joy of all. That is helping to lead someone to Christ - Every leader, every cook or maintenance or camp office worker, every parent, every pastor, every contributor that has helped one child spend time at camp has helped in that mission. The angels are singing!

Peace and Joy, Mr. Craig Giles, Summer Staff 1973-1997

The 1990s

The 1990s brought a change in leadership to Mar-Lu-ridge and a new direction.

1990-1991

Financial support continued to be a challenge. Land at the base of the mountain on the east side near the Three Ponds was surveyed and one tract was sold to generate needed funds.

1992

The Brohawn era at Mar-Lu-Ridge had come to an end. Executive Administrator Mr. Philip J. Brohawn retired and son, Director Stephen Lee Brohawn resigned.

1993 -1995

The Board called The Rev. LaVern Rasmussen to serve as Interim Executive Administrator. His primary task was to address issues expressed by pastors in the Synod. He met with them as a group, listened to their concerns, and then enlisted their efforts in turning a new page in

This photo shows Cabin #3, which was adopted by Zion Lutheran Church, Williamsport and named "The Huddle Hut" in honor of the Rev. William C. Huddle who served their congregation for 35 years.

The Rev. Lavern Rasmussen has served as Interim Administrator several times, keeping the camp focused and operational.

the history of MLR. Bishop George Mocko and The Rev. Albert Burkhardt were instrumental in securing and supporting Rasmussen.

John Bassett, now Manager at Mar-Lu-Ridge, who had gained experience in all aspects of the camp operation over many years, assumed a broader role which also included managing the office, finances, payroll, and facility use.

Over two and a half years the facilities were re-furbished by asking congregations to sponsor cabins for renovation. There were few funds available for maintenance. Volunteers and financial donors made it all possible. Two of the cabins were adopted by churches whose members took responsibility for the improvements: Cabin #3 was adopted by Zion, Williamsport and named the Huddle Hut in honor of their pastor, and Cabin #6 was adopted by Trinity, Taneytown.

New exterior steps were added to Lodge #3 as well as a new ceiling in the gathering room on the first floor. Interior furnishings were replaced in the Conference Center.

With renewed confidence, a search committee was assembled to select a new full-time Director.

On October 23, 1994, staff and friends of Mar-Lu-Ridge celebrated the 35th Anniversary at a service in the Chapel. The following are the words of invocation from that service. "Thank you Heavenly Father for the marvel of creation that surrounds us and for all the wonders of life you reveal to us. May our lives and Mar-Lu-Ridge be reawakened and renewed by the power of your grace."

"During the summer of 1996, the new director Rod Pearce quieted the lunch time crowd in Dining Hall #1 when he took a call from Frederick County Public Schools. Mr. Rod excitedly motioned me over to the phone where I was offered my first teaching job. My professional life finally launched at the place where I was inspired to enter it. At Mar-Lu-Ridge as a camper, I had found a place that fed my soul, and then as a counselor, through the encouragement of people like Mr. Craig Giles, I had found my calling as a teacher. Through the 1996-97 year, I experienced not only the pains of being a first year teacher, but I also suffered the loss of a close cousin. I decided to return to camp for the summer of 1997 even though I had an apartment and a full time job. Two of my other cousins again joined me on the Ridge; it was a summer of our grieving together while we worked hard to help Mr. Rod establish new traditions and renew a sense of safe fun and goofiness on the Ridge. Summer 1997 represented a difficult time of change that moved our camp and many of us toward the realization of a greater vision."

Beth Ziegler
Camper 1981-1987
Counselor 1991-93, 1996-98
Board Member 1998-2003

1996 - 1997

The Search Committee se-
lected Rod Pearce who began as
the new full-time Executive Director of Mar-Lu-Ridge effective
January 1. Rod had attended the
very first family camp at Mar-Lu-
Ridge, so he was quite excited to
return many years later as the
Director. Rod was instrumental in
getting MLR re-accredited by the
American Camping Association.

1998

Kris Brown was hired as Associate Director. He had been a

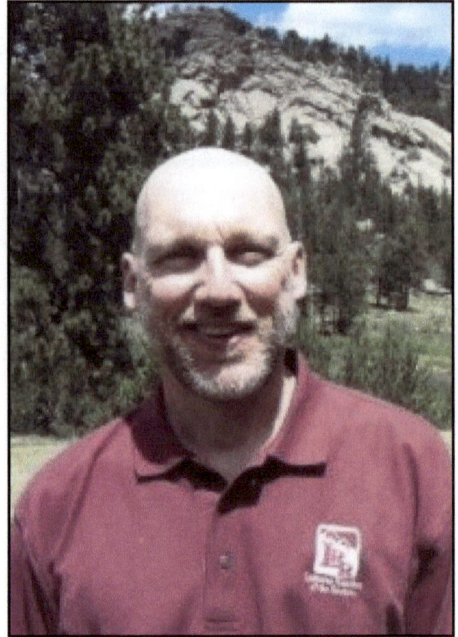

Rod Pearce served as Executive Director of
Mar-Lu-Ridge from 1996 - 2005.

camper and counselor at MLR for a combined total of 13 years and was
involved in music ministry.

Improvements were made to the Area #3 pond with the addition of a
new dock and the removal of algae and other plant material.

1999

More improvements to the cabins continued over the next five to six
years. These improvements included items such as new underground
electrical lines, refurbished bathrooms, drop ceilings, ceiling fans, new
floors, exterior repairs, etc.

The bathhouses in Area #3 were repaired, but will require replace-
ment in the near future.

A 40th Anniversary and Homecoming was celebrated with an activity
day complete with moon bounce, hiking, archery, face painting, and
singing.

The 2000s

The new millennium brought about many challenges for Mar-Lu-Ridge as it continued to find it's place in a fast-paced and ever changing world.

2000

Kris Brown left the position of Associate Director. He has since completed seminary at Gettysburg and is now an ordained pastor in Pennsylvania.

Nathan Pile replaced Kris Brown as Associate Director. Nathan was a religion major with lots of outdoor experience.

2001

Construction on the outdoor amphitheater began by clearing the selected site. That site is on the east side of the mountain not far from the turnaround above Dining Hall #1. Work was to continue on this project for the next four years.

A plan was initiated this year to increase the space available for recreational activities. The helipad was removed and over the next two years more than 75 truckloads of fill dirt were used to increase the available space.

2002

The first MLR day camp was held this summer at Area 3. Day camp is staffed by the MLR summer staff and day campers participate in all of the same activities as regular campers. This provides an opportunity for child care in a Christian community. It is popular with local working parents! The day camp continues to operate as of the writing of this history in the summer of 2009.

A number of changes took place in Area #3 this year. A three element high ropes course was built as the beginning phase of a group initiatives course. A new filtration system was installed in the Area #3 swimming pool, and both of the Area #3 ponds were restored to improve drainage and to increase water holding capacity.

The Three Ponds were also restored and new drainage pipes were installed.

The new amphitheater provides seating for 180 people. It is accessible via a path beginning at the camp road near the caboose.

2003

Nathan Pile left the position of Associate Director to return to Camp Sequanota to run their summer program He is now an ordained pastor in Pennsylvania.

Thomas Semeta was hired in March as Associate Director. He was a member of the MLR summer staff in 2001 and had worked at Lake Chautauqua Lutheran Center in New York before coming to MLR. He brought years of experience with Lutheran Outdoor Ministries to the position.

The animal pen was severely damaged by the effects of Hurricane Isabel which felled many trees on the Ridge. The damaged half was removed and the remaining portion restored for use.

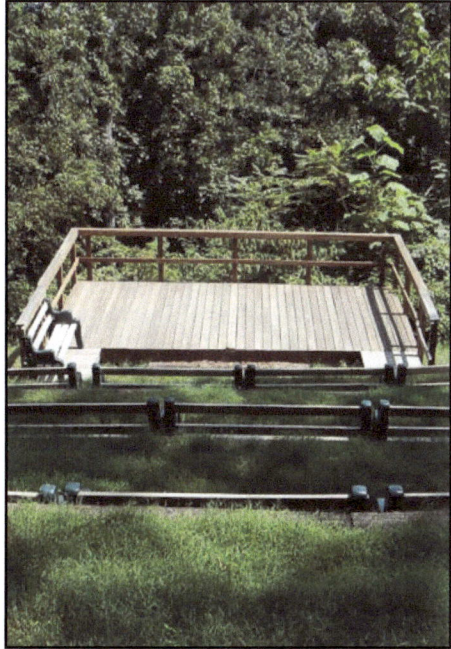

The new amphitheatre included a level stage area for use in the creative arts.

2004

The amphitheater begun in 2001 was nearly complete and ready for use. An access path to the amphitheater was made from the caboose across from DH #1. The amphitheater provides seating for 180 and has a 12' X 20' stage. Further enhancements were made in successive years.

A variety of improvements were made to Dining Hall #1, formerly named Lodge #1, the first building constructed at MLR. These improvements were made over a number of years with most of them completed by 2004. These included items such as tile, vertical blinds, cushioned chairs, ceiling fans, carpeting, and audio-visual equipment. Another name change is being considered since this building is now used primar-

The prayer labyrinth was constructed in 2005 and is used by summer campers as well as retreat groups throughout the year.

ily as a meeting and special events facility. Improvements to Lodge #3 were completed with carpeting and painting as the final steps. Upstairs rooms were air conditioned.

2005

A prayer labyrinth was constructed adjacent to the amphitheater. The prayer labyrinth, also known as a meditation labyrinth, is one of the oldest contemplative and transformational tools known, having been used for many hundreds of years for prayer, ritual, initiation, and spiritual growth. The prayer labyrinth was adopted by the Church across Europe during the medieval times, often being used as a means to meditate, pray, and connect with God in a higher spiritual way. It should be noted that the prayer labyrinth is not a *maze* in the popular sense and rather has a single path on which one cannot get lost, serving as a powerful symbol of individual life journeys and pilgrimage in faith.

After 45 years the "old wooden cross" was replaced with a "new wooden cross" and we pray that with God's blessing it will be a symbol of the camp for the next 45 years.

The animal pen, which had been at MLR since the 1960s and housed deer, chickens, goats, turkeys and ducks, was completely removed. The animals were given to a petting zoo. This was the end of an era for MLR.

Three new elements were added to the group initiatives course in Area #3 increasing the total to six.

2006

Mar-Lu-Ridge factoid - It costs an average of $1800 a day to operate Mar-Lu-Ridge. This comes to about $75 an hour or $1.25 per minute.

2007

For 24 hours beginning on January 27, something happened at Mar-Lu-Ridge that hasn't happened in 45 years – there was no cross in front of Salem-on-the-Mountain Chapel. It took just 10 minutes to remove this symbol of the mission of Mar-Lu-Ridge that has served as a waypoint for pilots on their way to Dulles Airport and had been the centerpiece of thousands of photographs since 1962. The deteriorating 45 year old cross was replaced the next morning with a new, one ton solid white oak cross. This stunning and sturdy new cross is a beacon of hope and glory for all. Thanks to Keith Schoonover of Good Shepherd Lutheran Church in Frederick for making the new cross.

This was another year of change and transition. Thomas Semeta left the position of Associate Director and was replaced by Andrew Rickel in May. He had already been an avid member of the Mar-Lu-Ridge community for many years prior to that. He had been an MLR camper and summer staff member. He came to Mar-Lu-Ridge after graduating from Lenoir-Rhyne College in North Carolina. He was very excited to be a part of this ministry!

Rod Pearce resigned as Executive Director this year to accept a position in Colorado as Director of Lutheran Ranches of the Rockies, and once again Rev. LaVern Raamussen was hired as Interim Director, this time only for six months.

A Search Committee, chaired by Rev. Art Cubbon, was formed and selected Derrick Trautman as the new Executive Director. He had previously served Camp Frederick in Easter, Ohio.

2008

MLR entered into a three-way Capital Funds Campaign with Gettysburg Seminary and the Delaware-Maryland Synod. Representatives of each partnership provided direction from a management team. The effort continues until 2010.

This year marked the first offsite day camp. In this program interested churches contract with MLR to provide a day camp experience at their church. MLR summer staff travel to the church and live at the church site for that week while providing all of the camp activities.

2009

Derrick Trautman resigned in order to accept a position with the Department of the Army as Director of the Youth Center at Ft. Meade, Maryland. His resignation was effective July 31.

Sarah Lefler and Rev. LaVern Rasmussen were asked to step in and be the management team for one year. They agreed to serve virtually as volunteers in an effort to reestablish a financial foundation for MLR. Many solid Mar-Lu-Ridgers offered support. This is a year of rebuilding and rethinking traditional ways of doing outdoor ministry.

The main activity of this year is a capital funds campaign in the Metropolitan Washington D.C. Synod of the ELCA. The consulting firm of Gronlund, Sayther and Brunkow was hired with Jim Cunningham as the on-site consultant. The Rev. Tom Omholt is the Campaign Chair. Members of the committee will attempt to visit all congregations during the year, encouraging each to conduct a pre-designed solicitation effort. Bishop Richard Graham is Chair of the Congregational Phase of the campaign.

One of the tasks of the MLR Financial Development Committee is to seriously seek increased financial support from the two supporting Synods. User fees are inadequate to support the Ministry. Grants and donations are essential. The Financial Development Committee is beginning a new giving club - Vision of the Ridge Giving Club. Everyone is an essential component to furthering the success, traditions, and growth of Mar-Lu-Ridge. Suggested levels of giving are as follows:

Mountaintoppers – As our Mission says, "Mar-Lu-Ridge offers a mountaintop Experience." As the pinnacle of annual giving, the *Mountaintopper category* was established to recognize those contributors donating $5000 or more to the Mar-Lu-Ridge ministry.

Ridge Runners – Ridge runner is a term for mountain climber. Recognizing those who provide annual support of $1000 to $5000, the *Ridge Runners* provide the funds necessary for continued growth.

Star Reachers – There are those who look toward the sky and dream – those who realize the potential of our ministry. The *Star Reachers* motivate us to dream by contributing between $500 and $999 annually.

Ascenders – In mountain climbing an ascender is a device that provides safety from falling while assisting the climber to move upward. The *Ascenders* provide the funds required to begin our climb with donations of $250 to $499.

Ridge Climbers - Includes all who support the ministry of Mar-Lu-Ridge with a gift of $100 to $249 – providing the rock upon which our ministry is built.

Junior High campers work as a group preparing for their cookout in this July 1978 photo.

From my first encounter as a camper in the mid-60s, and for summers to come as a staff member, I always felt that Mar-Lu-Ridge would remain as a part of my life. So, here it is over 40 years later, and many of us are still gathering at the Ridge every summer to maintain our friendships and keep our MLR memories alive. God has truly blessed this wonderful place.

Laura Tegge Higgs

Former Camper and Summer Staff Member

*Small Group Camping
and the
Mar-Lu-Ridge Experience*

Throughout the last fifty years, the camping philosophy at Mar-Lu-Ridge has focused on the idea of small group camping. While each area of the camp could hold as many as 60 campers or more, each area was divided into smaller groups, averaging about 15 campers per group. These small groups ate together, slept together, hiked together, and did chores together.

Each group created special bonds amongst themselves and was a unique entity. The small groups provided an atmosphere that was particularly conducive to making new friendships and renewing old ones and it was not uncommon for campers to keep in touch throughout the year and reunite for a special week at camp. Each summer it would be these small groups that would bring life to the Ridge and make it a vibrant place to live and to learn about God in our world.

Each week was unique, as different campers would come and go.

This undated photo (probably late 1970s) shows a small group in front of the Mar-Lu-Ridge sign as you enter Area #1.

A busy Sunday afternoon as parents and campers arrive at Area #3 during the summer of 1974.

Until recent years the camping week started on Sunday afternoon and ended on Saturday morning. These times were very hectic times as campers came and went. The first few hours of camp were always filled with a little anxiety as campers tried to familiarize themselves with new surroundings and as parents hugged and kissed their children good-bye.

For many years nametags were made by the campers using chipped wood blocks and macaroni letters. It was a fun craft and a great way to get to learn everybody's name. Once all the campers had arrived, parents were heading home, and nametags were made, it was off to the first meal of the week.

There were many mainstays to the camping week and meals were a top priority for many a growing camper. Breakfast, lunch and dinner were served throughout the week. Breakfast always began at 8:00 am, lunch was served at noon and dinner was eaten at 5:00 pm. Mealtimes were fun times. Campers were particularly fond of the singing that was done after each meal. As was tradition, whichever group had the chore of setting the tables for the day also had the fun of picking which songs to sing.

To help orient the campers to the spiritual aspect of the camp, the week always started with a worship service and ended with a worship service. Campers, under the direction of the group leaders, conducted these services each week. There was always a mid-week service as well, most often held on Wednesday, and the location would vary. The Sunday evening service was usually already prepared by the camp staff and campers were asked to take part in the readings of scripture or the announcement of songs. However, the mid-week worship and the Saturday worship had no boundaries and the brilliance of the worship was only limited by the creativity of the campers.

Chores were also a part of each day. Typical chores included dining hall, bathrooms, grounds, tables and barn. If your group was responsible for dining hall, that meant you had to clean the hall after breakfast which included sweeping and mopping the floors as well as cleaning the bath-

This photo from the summer of 1981 shows one of the many closing worship services held in the outdoor chapel in Area #2. Parents who arrived early enough were able to see their children participate in the worship service.

This photo shows junior campers enjoying a lunchtime meal in Dining Hall 3 during the summer of 1968.

rooms. If you were responsible for bathrooms, you had to clean "the johns" as they were so often called. Grounds meant that you were to police the area and pick up any trash that may have been accidentally discarded by campers or parents. Having tables as your chore, meant that you had to set the tables prior to each meal. The barn was a particular chore for Area 3 campers, and it simply meant that you had to clean and straighten the barn.

Each day after breakfast camp council was held to decide the week's events. Typically two campers and one leader from each group would attend the council and would then relay decisions that the group as a whole had already made. In the very early days camp council was held in a teepee. As the years went by, camp council would be held near the fire circle in Area 2 or in the barn in Area 3. One of the biggest decisions each group had to make was whether they wanted to have small group activities or large group activities. Usually each week was blend of both small and large group activities. Most campers were eager to be a camp

This early and undated image shows a small group identifying the mountaintop foliage in front of the camp council teepee.

council representative in order to be a part of this important decision making process; however, many campers just wanted to get out of doing chores. Especially if the chore for the day was the johns!

There were many activities for the groups to choose from when it came to deciding the week's events. Swim olympics, mock olympics, movie night, and the traditional weekly dance were among the many choices available.

Other activities that could be done by the individual groups were hiking, games, crafts, and sleep outs. There were numerous places to hike including the power lines, the three ponds, the peddler's grave, or even to one of the other areas. Junior High campers would trek down the mountain from Area 1 or Area 2 to Area 3 and Junior campers from Area 3 would hike up the mountain to Areas 1 and 2. In many cases, groups would spend the night in the area to which they hiked. It was not uncommon to find groups sleeping at the helipad or in the barn at any point during the week. These hikes between the areas gave the small group a

This undated photo depicts a successful hike to the power lines from junior camp Area 3.

great sense of pride and accomplishment.

Hikes to special areas such as the peddler's grave always gave rise to story telling. The story of the peddler and his one true love, Aggie, has been a longtime tradition at camp. Of course, there are as many versions of the story as there have been counselors on the Ridge. It was never told the same way twice.

Another staple to each weekday at camp was the beloved swim time. From 1:30 to 4:30 each afternoon, groups would take turns swimming in one of the two pools at Mar-Lu-Ridge. During the hot days of July and August, afternoon swimming was the highlight of the day for hundreds of campers. While the shade of the towering trees offered some refuge from the heat, there was nothing quite like jumping in the pool. Sometimes the campers would participate in a night swim, and swim after dinner instead of before dinner.

For many campers swim time was followed by rest time. Rest time was a time to write home and tell mom and dad what was going on, how

Swim Olympics was just one of the many activities where groups competed against one another. This photo shows a Junior High Swim Olympics from the summer of 1979.

much fun you were having, and how much you couldn't wait to see them. It was also a time to gather with your new found friends and talk about what you had in common or which of the girls or guys in your group was the cutest.

Each day would also consist of morning and evening devotions as well as a Bible lesson or Bible study. These lessons were done at any time of the day and usually emphasized a particular theme for the week. Campers were always expected to bring a Bible, a pencil, and paper to camp to use for the daily lessons.

One of the many traditions that evolved over the last fifty years was that of the Thursday night dance. When the dance tradition started in the early 1970s, it was held in the pavilion across from the chapel. Over time it had to be moved to Lodge #2 because the vibrations from the music and the dancing in the pavilion was causing rust and dirt to fall into the 50,000 gallon water holding tank which was located directly under the pavilion.

Another tradition at Mar-Lu-Ridge was that of the weekly cookout. Once a week the camp cooks were given an afternoon off and the groups prepared and ate their own dinner. Hobo dinners, corn on the cob, BBQ chicken, and ice cream were staple items for many small group cookouts at Mar-Lu-Ridge.

Another weekly ritual was the taking of the camp picture. Mr. Kodak as he was so fondly known, would come to the various camp areas and take photos of all camps that were in session. Campers would purchase their picture at the end of the week, and many campers would have their friends sign the back of the picture. The picture was then taken home as a memento of another great week at camp.

At some point during the camping week a time was set aside for some good old fashioned arts and crafts. Macramé bracelets, necklaces, and belts were a long standing tradition for much of the 1960s and 1970s. When the 1980s were ushered in, the cotton string used for mac-ramé was replaced by a plastic lace affectionately called gimp. Count-

A small Junior High group gathered around the picnic tables for the daily lesson.

This photo shows one of the first traditional Junior High dances held during the summer of 1970.

less campers went home with plastic bracelets, rings, hair ties, key chains and more made from gimp. Of course, other crafts such as matchstick crosses, ice candles, and other arts made from natural material were created as well.

Music and singing have been a part of the Mar-Lu-Ridge tradition since the earliest days of the camp. Many a camper rode home with their parents on Saturday morning or Friday evening still singing their favorite song of the week. While some songs were just meant to be sung, other songs were meant to be acted out as well. This usually led to a riotous finale at any given meal.

Asking campers about their week was usually the trigger for a 45 minute dissertation on the hikes they had taken and how they got lost, how many different dives they did in the swimming pool, who won mock olympics, and why they shouldn't have won, how they danced every dance on Thursday night, how there were so many creepy spiders in the arks, and how they couldn't wait to get a good night's sleep.

Mar-Lu-Ridge
Summer Staff
Photos

Summer Staff 1964

Summer Staff 1966

Summer Staff 1967

Summer Staff 1968

Summer Staff 1969

Summer Staff 1970

Summer Staff 1971

Summer Staff 1972

Summer Staff 1973

Summer Staff 1974

Summer Staff 1975

Summer Staff 1976

Summer Staff 1977

Summer Staff 1978

Summer Staff 1979

Summer Staff 1980

Summer Staff 1981

Summer Staff 1982

Summer Staff 1983

Summer Staff 1984

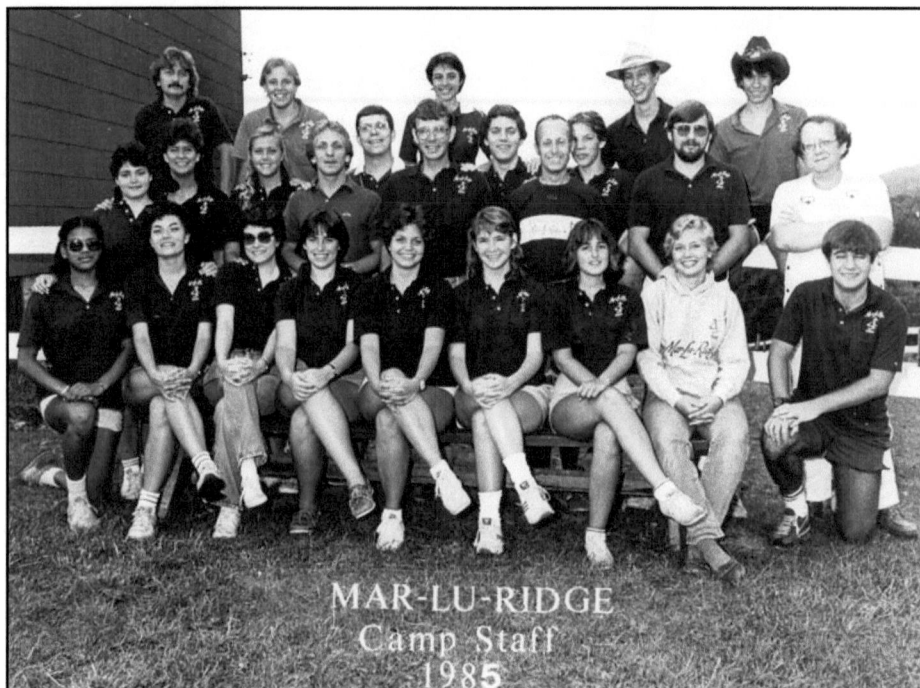

Summer Staff 1985

Summer Staff 1986

Summer Staff 1987

Summer Staff 1988

Summer Staff 1989

Summer Staff 1990

Summer Staff 1991

Summer Staff 1992

Summer Staff 1993

Summer Staff 1994

Summer Staff 1995

Summer Staff 1996

Summer Staff 1997

Summer Staff 1998

Summer Staff 1999

Summer Staff 2000

Summer Staff 2001

Summer Staff 2002

Summer Staff 2003

Summer Staff 2004

Summer Staff 2005

Summer Staff 2006

Summer Staff 2009

About the Editors

Philip Brohawn has been involved in the workings of Mar-Lu-Ridge since the early 1960s. His experience with the camp has ranged from lifeguard to camp counselor to program director. Philip has lived on the Ridge since his family moved there in 1960 where he has watched and helped the camp grow for the last fifty years. His knowledge of the camp and its history has been vital to the creation of this book. Outside of the camp, Philip has recently retired from the Frederick County School System where he served as a teacher and science curriculum specialist for 37 years.

Craig Schenning has been involved with Mar-Lu-Ridge since the mid -1970s. His experience with the camp has ranged from camper to counselor to area coordinator. Craig was also involved with the repair and maintenance of the facilities during the 1980s and later served on the board of directors. Craig's love and familiarity with the camp has made him an ideal candidate to help in the creation of this book. Outside of the camp, Craig worked as an environmental chemist for 20 years before opening his own publishing company in 2006.

www.ingramcontent.com/pod-product-compliance
Lightning Source LLC
Chambersburg PA
CBHW051238090426
42742CB00001B/10